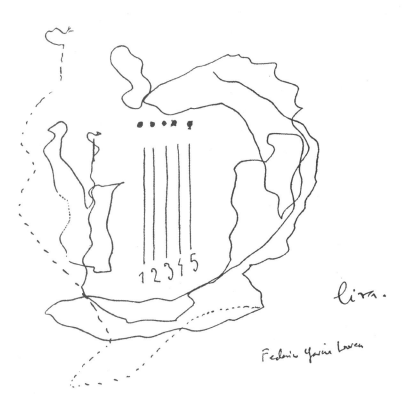

lira.

Federico Garcia Lorca

HYDROLOGOS

Warren Heiti

To Fred,

with good wishes
for your poetic work.

WH

PEDLAR PRESS | Toronto

Waterloo, May 2012

ACKNOWLEDGEMENTS
The publisher wishes to thank the Canada Council for the Arts and the Ontario Arts Council for their generous support of our publishing program.

Drawing by Federico García Lorca, *Lira / Lyre*, copyright © Herederos de Federico García Lorca. Excerpt by Federico García Lorca copyright © Herederos de Federico García Lorca. Translation by Christopher Maurer. All rights reserved. For information regarding rights and permissions please contact lorca@artslaw.co.uk or William Peter Kosmas, Esq., 8 Franklin Square, London W14 9UU, England.

LIBRARY AND ARCHIVES CANADA
CATALOGUING IN PUBLICATION

Heiti, Warren, 1979-
        Hydrologos / Warren Heiti.

Poems.
ISBN 978-1-897141-43-4

   I. Title.

PS8615.E38H93 2011   C811'.6   C2011-904312-2

COVER ART *Tafoni* by Larry Foden

EDITED FOR THE PRESS by Jan Zwicky

DESIGN Zab Design & Typography, Toronto

TYPEFACE Walbaum

Printed in Canada

ONTARIO ARTS COUNCIL
CONSEIL DES ARTS DE L'ONTARIO

THE CANADA COUNCIL | LE CONSEIL DES ARTS
FOR THE ARTS | DU CANADA
SINCE 1957 | DEPUIS 1957

An agency of the Government of Ontario

I ask God to grant me strength and joy (yes joy!) so that
I can write this book ... of devotion for those who travel
through the desert ...

— FEDERICO GARCÍA LORCA

HYDROLOGOS

1
11 OFELIA

2
27 THE UNCOLLECTED WORKS OF SALLIE CHISUM

3
41 THE METAMORPHOSIS OF AGRIOPE

4
73 THE SAME RIVER

5
85 HAREY'S PRAYERS

Coda
95 RAIN SUTRA

104 *Notes*

108 *Acknowledgements*

HYDROLOGOS

OFELIA

Water motifs, which symbolised the passage of time,
became a common element in painting and in graphics;
a sheet of water was a homologue of the soul.

— STEFANIA KOZAKOWSKA

Rain

pollinates
everything. The poppies
against a background
of dry grass, the first stars
in their burlap. Sand soda potash
a sheet of stained glass
smashed on the landscape.

And, after the rain,
the burden of crickets,
tuning their wings and beginning
their allegro elegy, angry
double basses pumping out trochees,
beige and beige and beige and beige and
into this, out of the eavestrough,
drop two tentative notes:

blue,

blue.

Your eyes,
their counterpoint with time.

Sleep

I live on Fitzroy Road, at the intersection with the Street of
Crocodiles, the ghetto where they smoke heroin. I have been
tending my rectangle of dirt. Columbine, campion, pansy,
daisy, rosemary, rue, orchid, violet, nettle, fennel. Pansies
and rosemary, thought and memory. The young woodcutter
crosses the bridge, his face pale as poplar bark, the moon
perched on his shoulder, in one hand a torch, in the other an
axe, ochre with sap. I have the horseshoe. I have the nails.

There is one knife of sunlight, lengthening, on the wall. The
knives of the vine flatten themselves on the anvil of autumn.
The peace lily's little ivory gloves are quivering to the
rhythm of *Boléro* or the breeze coming in the window; some
of the leaves are corroded, chlorophyll stilettos. The red
satellites of the crabapple tree tremble and threaten to break
the false laws of gravity. The maples were my timepiece.
I said, if they go yellow, I have failed. Wrist bone, broken
stem. My heart the sundial's xanthic hand, fallen in the grass.
I have the horseshoe, I have the nails, I have the hourglass
and exactly two minutes and twenty seconds of sand.

On the axis of the scarecrow's arm, Munin mourns Hugin.
Memory and thought. A background of maple and crabapple
leaves, crossed by the voice of a crow: olive, mauve — coal.
In my rented room the Sinfonia Varsovia is descending
through the varied shades of blue. I live on Fitzroy Road.
Indigo, indigo. Black sun, rusted moon. Poppy, opium,
laudanum, morphine, heroin. A genealogy.

Gold

I have only the one
photograph of you.
The one I chose. You
cannot be more than ten years old,
your back against a flaking
plaster wall, the fierce —
or is it plaintive? —
look in your eye, half
your face eclipsed, and the raw
umber sun blazing across the frame.
Your mind was like that, a full-blown
aperture, a fast shutter, flooded
with light from the spectrum
of the wasp, złoty, golden.
The body at five o'clock
and the mind already five
thousand million years old.

Your paintings were irradiated
by the same alien light.
I remember it, abstracted
from all that I cannot remember.
It was the very idea
of light, vespertine
and precise, reflected
on the retina of your mind,

the gold bands divided
from the black and alchemized
into twenty-four carat
fire and graphite. But
sterile.

The mind is moored to others;
the wasps orbit on little tethers of light.

Scorpion

You are the scorpion of rust who scuttled into my boot while
I slept. Yesterday you brought me the fallen sparrow, its
driftwood wings, the stops of its throat, whittled by termites.
In your other claw, the honey jar with the larva, a stamen
paralysed in amber. There is the scar where they removed
the wasp from my abdomen. You smell of ether, you whisper
your hypothermia into my ear, you distil your argentine
accent, your rubious vocabulary. My saliva thickens with
sickness. When I wake, you have withered my violets with
your piss. I lie with my cheek against your silver thorax
and you stroke my hair, you feed me leather bullets, the
embalmed bodies of cicadas, raisins. Your fingers blur my
lips. Mute, I stumble through the dry, verdigris aqueducts
of your eye, thinking this prayer, formic acid, ant spit and
sandpaper: blink and I will be expelled, sharpen the edge of
the water, subtract me from eternity.

Death

You hold my index finger in your fist,
whisper that you were eating candy
when they told you about your father's death —
I have learned many words in English
but I cannot describe it: the taste
of the candy, the barking
of the dog. My hearts
are blown from green and brown
glass, solar winds
drone across the aortal necks.
The clock above the bar stretches out
its empty hands. Is there
no consolation? There is
the moving constellation
on the pool table. The appendix
pickled in alcohol, the gangrenous toe.
The tackle box behind the bar. Two
dimes beside the salt shaker.

The waitress is stacking milk crates like plastic
rib cages. I hear my hearts
rattling in her hands, I see the sex
of her skeleton, her scapulae and clavicles
flexing. She
exhales, and extends
the four membranes of her wings, laced
with brittle capillaries, and bends

her mosaic gaze upon me:
the dragonfly's dodecahedron, the ten thousand
manifestations.

The iris of your fist
constricts.

Blue

The rule of distance: blue. The woman combing out her hair as though she is inclined across a harp, the trajectory of her arm: red. Yellow: a mental illness.

My mouth was brass when the taxi took you to the airport. If I can't touch you, what words will I use? *Biały*, white: your home, seagulls and snow. While you were away, I walked into the ocean and gathered white shells, one for each day. A heron waited with me, its eye baited with star. When you came back, sane, I broke the shells and gave them back to the ocean.

A black man empties a carton of milk into the bird tracks cemented in the sidewalk. Beneath the speed limit sign, a woman's pair of red shoes, as though she stepped out of them and into the wavelength of brake lights, receding. You laughed, tearing lobsters with your bare hands. The moon, a thumbprint, a whirlpool of blue.

Time is violent, yellow, elliptical. At the centre of time is a mind made of hydrogen and helium and rabies. Amnesia is a disease, it means you are illuminated by the blue light of the Carpathian Mountains, it means a knife in the bathtub of cheap red wine. The violence is mine, I am the one who needs to be forgiven.

Niebieski, blue: grief, the blood heaves through the cobalt

veins, the vacancies resonate with rain. I have waited all

evening, you are there on the corner, your skates laced over

your shoulder. My mouth was brass, your ear was glass,

mirror dimly mirroring. Grief, I know, hears only itself.

Listen: the solstice of the mind.

Tlaloc

When I could not read
and I could not eat
and I could not sleep, when sleep
was sealed behind two weeks of glass,
and the wind was thin with my mind,
and my mind was
carbon monoxide, you
came to me, Tlaloc,
you came in a box, inert
whirlwind, white room
that walled in my insomnia,
and you loomed over me, your divining rod
riveted to my temple, and you
bent down and seized my soul by the hair and cracked its spine
like a whip
and the cataracts of your knowledge
crashed into my skull. Convulsed, I knew

the name of the father of the rain, the name
of the heron who gave
her feathers for your crown,
knew the concentric circles
of your eyes, their blue nuclei, knew
the contents of your four
jars, the storehouses
of hail, bile and bees,

could read the kinesis
of the lightning, the fibres
of the bolt, the body
of your body, the knots
in the wood, the rhythm
jagged, impacted
and rising,
a tree of fire, rising
through the canalized sky,
one leg grounded and the pinioned
hands, the fifty phalanxes
shredding the net of clouds. I knew
the February of my death,
the moment when the lungs would fill
with mind, its satellite
whiteness, and the electrons of flesh end
their stupid orbit around the one
sun, Aldebaran, red eye
of Hyades.

All this I knew while you
held me, an embryo
in the hands of elm,
while you stroked
the salt oracles
out of my sockets;
and when you dropped me
onto the hard bed,
narcotized, ossified, I
had forgotten
all.

Hourglass

Music is monophonic. Light is fibrous. When you left for
Poland, you said you would bring back the wedding bands.
You brought back an hourglass. Time is a symptom of music
and light.

The afternoon sun filters through the yellow fabric of
the curtains. I have been listening to the radio. Van den
Budenmayer, the composer, played billiards, alone, with a
notebook. The white cue ball was his mind. The size of a
point. Dimensionless.

The second dimension, the first shape: a triangle, its three
vertices riveted with stars.

I remember adjusting my glove at the exit, and adjusting it
again, then leaving and pausing on the landing while the
two doors thudded behind me, first the second door, then
the first. Holding my gloved hand to my lips.

From the first three dimensions, abstract the fourth. This is
what memory means: geometry: dream.

Somewhere I am standing in line to purchase a marriage
licence. The carpets patched with duct tape, the couple
in front of me bickering in Spanish, somebody rapping a
typewriter, somebody calling my name.

The radio fills the room with solids. The sun angles through the shattered glass and sand. I dream, briefly, of you with your pool cue, curved over the green felt plane. There are six pockets — one of them is your heart.

The taste of chalk. The sun lays its copper thumbs on my eyelids. The radio plays the monologue of a dog. What is the formula for tomorrow?

THE UNCOLLECTED WORKS OF SALLIE CHISUM

Then the certainties he loathed and needed were liquid at
the root.

— MICHAEL ONDAATJE

Billy shaved off his moustache
in my bathroom and now he's
smoking his corncob pipe
the coral of his spine braced
against the snarled bark
of the vine   he breathes
serene   bullets washed up
around his bare feet

And Garrett's resting on my bed
in his yellow raincoat
the oranges turning to cork
on the bookshelf and the sky
scraped pure as an oyster shell
with its purple whorl —

    (After that we drifted I guess
I went west   Garrett
went to the red sands
in the east   Billy
went to the centre   lived
under a wrecked sky)

28

Henry stares and stares thru
me and I crouch on the kitchen
floor and stare at him till
my nose itches and I cant
hear I cant hear nothing but
I can smell me and I can
smell the musk of the buckskin
jacket and the tan of my own
skin and I can smell the angels'
piss around the property
yes their piss stinks like
whisky   wasnt that the name
of the Doberman whose owner
once cut my hair   yes the dog
was Whisky and his ears
hadnt been cut   Henry

        clatters into another room
the noise of his nails on the floor
jerking me back into this kitchen
and thru the porch door I hear
the faraway gearing of stars
and in the hallway the clock
is ticking backwards

The cuckoo crying
in twenty-one circles
and its cry is in my
chest

Billy played the didjeridoo
like a long wooden throat
his breath coming
from the carved mouth
by his bare foot and circling
back into his nostrils

Saying the word star the word
water into the didjeridoo
white circles of water
and stars squawking
from his wooden mouth

Pointing with his pale left hand
and saying   I blew those
termites from my horn
and the stars squirming
under his ivory fingernail

Billy putting down the didjeridoo
and smoking on the porch
so quiet I could hear the leaves
burning when he breathed in
and his nose hair whistling
when he breathed out

Before sunrise one morning Garrett hammers at my back door, shouts, Open up Sallie it's the law. When I do he's got shattered oranges in his hands, juice on his bare forearms and mouth and his shirt is all stained. What're you doing here Garrett it's four in the morning and I havent seen you since the burial. He says, I need to talk to you about Billy.

What about Billy, I ask. I had a nightmare about the angels, he says. I had to squint to look at them they were so bright, some of them held me to a bunk and some of them looked me over and then one of them says, YOU'RE SICK SHERIFF, YOU'VE GOT IT BAD, says, THERE ARE TWO CURES FOR WHAT AILS YOU, SURGERY OR DEATH, and I says, I'm not sick, and the angel says, DON'T FUCK AROUND, LOOK AT YOUR WRISTS THEY'RE RUSTING WHERE THEY STICK OUT OF YOUR SLEEVES, LOOK AT THE RUST BLEEDING THRU YOUR BREAST POCKET, says, THERE ARE TWO CURES, and I says, I heard you already, cut it out of me then like I know you want to, and they open a jug of gasoline and pour it into my mouth and I have a hell of a time getting it down, Sallie I aint been drunk in over one hundred and twenty-five years but I got real drunk on that gasoline, and then that angel tears my shirt and grabs a scalpel and goes to work on my chest, and let me tell you that sure felt peculiar, and when he's done he wipes his hands on a rag and then he holds this thing up to the light and says, THERE SHERIFF THAT'S YOUR FUSE YOU CAN SEE WHERE THE ELECTRICITY HAS FRIED THE GLASS. And I says, You got any spares? And the angels get a big kick out of that. And then I woke up and was real hungry for oranges but when I ate them they all tasted like gasoline. And I came round to see if you got any. You got any oranges Sallie?

31

(In her dream   Garrett's in the yard
yanking rattlers   lightning bolts
out of the limbs of birch

They spark and corkscrew
around his forearms
and around his ankles
in circles   uncertainly
canters the dust)

Billy comes to me under the oak tree

where I'm biting the blackberry

thorns out of my thumbs

He gives me a bullet

he found on the gulf shore

tells me he

aims to marry Angela D

A crow moans and scratches

its beak on the branch

above me   shits purple

on my left hand holding

the bullet   and all of a sudden

the lead gleams dim

blue   like the steel

of an angel's tooth

Meanwhile

cobwebs

cut up

the sky

She was rinsing
tomatoes under the tap
when the angel fell
thru the porch roof
its arm a fleshless length
of star   the quills
of light razoring out
along the sixteen wings
and the wings within wings
and the atoms splintering
in the aluminum cranium

The voice loveless as the voice
of God   PROPHET   YOU
ARE CALLED   YOU
WILL BE BALD   YOUR
LIPS WILL BE CIRCUMCISED
WITH LIVE COAL   YOU
WILL INGEST A SCROLL INSCRIBED
WITH THE HOLY EQUATION   LOVE
= OBEDIENCE   YOU
WILL BE PURIFIED
BY FIRE

34

Its scimitar arm
shone   its helicopter limbs
shone   its nuclear eye-sockets
shone   its cerebrum
crunched another atom

It salivated battery acid
she noticed the neon corona
bolted to the atmosphere
around its skull   it held out
a blowtorch and offered to fix
her broken
soul

No
thanks she said but you
can fix that hole
in my porch roof

Sitting with Henry on the back porch
wearing one of John's white shirts
hot as noon at eight AM but quiet
tho Henry's hearing things I cant hear
I can tell cause his ears are twitching
I blow steam from the milk and tea
and still burn my mouth   pour a tumbler
full of ice and whisky   get up
go to the porch rail and brush the dead
leaves from the smothered datura

There is a man whose mouth I sometimes
want   this tumbler of whisky better
than the first   it's harsher
hotter   days as hard as the glass
tumbler against the wood rail

A loose shirt and too many tumblers
of whisky   the man whose mouth
I sometimes want has left   he came close
enough so I could feel   so I could
feel   so I could hear   did he hear
he came close enough so I could hear
his heat   he came close enough   did he
hear   he came close enough   a loose
shirt   I heard his heat   too many
tumblers of whisky   and I want
his mouth   warm was the first time
warm was the first time   warm was
the first time I felt   but who's counting

warm was warm was warm was
warm was a man whose mouth I always wanted
and warm was a man who is not warm
and warm was what I remembered when I felt
the heat of his hand   when I felt
the heat of his hand thru my white
cotton shirt

Sitting with Henry on the back porch
wearing one of John's white shirts
smoking and plucking loose tobacco
and tea leaves from my lips and thinking
about you Billy   crows cool the sky
with their flight   but my shadow's
thin as my shirt and the sun
goes straight thru   whitens
my white shirt and turns
the wood of the rail
to wood

Eclipse and the Pleiades hang
like a filigree earring
from the lobe of Ethiopia
and Garrett murmurs *the earth*
is like a garden spider
in some large dark
house

They're playing mancala at the table
he gathers his stones and sows
them across the board   seven
deer step across the dead cornfield

The web of the Milky Way stretched
taut as latticed steel across
the ceiling

He chews his wine-tipped cigar   his tin star
unpinned and hidden in his chest
pocket but she can hear it throbbing
like a pulsar in the dark

She puts her fingertips on his wrist
but his pulse is a stopped watch
and the purple birthmark spills
into her lap   stains her skirt

A rotten orange   a toppled
wineglass   a spider climbing
the stars

THE METAMORPHOSIS
OF AGRIOPE

She was already loosened like long hair
and given over like fallen rain
and handed out like a limitless supply.

She was already root.

— RAINER MARIA RILKE

Georgics, Book 4

The bees were dying and it would not rain
and Aristaios had read a book bound
in snake leather that said one could get
a hive of bees from the guts of a bull.
He brought the only bull to the bay
and he cut the bull's throat and went
and squatted by the water and smoked
and waited until he heard the sun's drone.
And Aristaios knew that nine dawns
had passed and he turned to the bull's corpse
and slit its stomach and dragged out its guts,
and the guts were honeycombed and humming.
He knew that the sounds inside
were yellow and black, the rasp of sick leaves,
and now he had a handful of autumn
and a dead bull, but it would not rain, still,
and still Agriope was dead. And the bull,
its lips and nostrils black with nine dawns
of rot, began to yell. Aristaios
looked from the hive in his hands to the bull
and the black rapids charging from its mouth
towards the sea. It was too late. By night
the sea would be wracked with gangrene.
Aristaios felt the hive fall silent
in his hands and knew that it would
not rain. And he sat down in the sand
and cut open the hive and took each bee
into his mouth.

Metamorphoses, Book 5

Persephone is picking narcissi, roses, crocuses, violets,
irises, hyacinths and narcissi by the chain-link fence when
she sees Haides.

He is handsome and smells like wealth. The narcissus
petals are nickel-white, pale as his shadow. They scatter in
the gravel and parched grass as she falls.

She wakes in an empty room. Concrete walls, concrete floor,
no windows. She is naked, face down, her wrists shackled
behind her back, the long chain locked to an iron ring in the
centre of the floor. There is a china plate in
the corner.

When she resists, he strangles her with the chain.

She learns to be inert. The door opens, the fluorescent
overheads flicker on. When he is finished, he places a single
garnet on the plate, flicks out the lights, closes the door. She
has no sense of the intervals, but has counted seven garnets.

43

She is now starving. In the dark she drags herself along
the radius of the chain. She bends to the plate and takes a
garnet into her mouth. Her flesh hardens to gem.

Homeric Hymn to Demeter

Demeter segregates herself in the temple of her dignified grief. In her left hand is an ear of corn, in her right is a sheaf of wheat. The corn is the colour of the wheat and the wheat is the colour of concrete. The kernels of corn are gravel teeth clenched in a grin and the stalagmite of wheat came from grains of wind-sown stone. The ear was reaped in silence, in silence the wheat had been sheaved.

She fasts for nine days and on the ninth Agriope brings her a glass of barley water flavoured with pennyroyal. Demeter spits the water in Agriope's face: *This loss belongs to me.* She hoards it like a body hoarding fat, she fattens herself on famine, her uncountable udders calcify with milk. And after Agriope has left, she digs into her tear ducts and finds the seeds of winter, white as dandelion seeds, and gives them to the wind.

When Agriope returns, in the season of hail, Demeter nurses her with aether, and she takes Agriope's mind and hides it in the fire, and time begins to burn off, like dew from a spiderweb. And Agriope begins to forget the wasted fields she walked through, the suppliants starving in camps around the temple. The last thing she remembers is Persephone's belt, floating in the water — and she wrenches her mind out of the fire.

Inferno, Canto 13

After some bad months, the season of amnesia,
Agriope finds herself in a shadowed wood,
the lake of her heart closed, her feet clothed
with sand from the beaches of the Lethe,
the melanin-skinned sun
mute in the trees, in the pallid branches
and black leaves where crows
with women's faces rake
the bark with their teeth
and shit their white shit
on the dry ground. Near a dead riverbed
are two bare trees, a willow and a yew, and the crows
do not approach them. The willow's bark is rotten
and water has scalded and scarred the bark of the yew,
and their shadows like strangling vines grasp and couple
with their trunks. Agriope pauses here
and the crows scowl at her, showing their bilious gums,
and rearrange the wrecked foliage of their wings.
She hears a hiss, the prison song of steam,
and places her palm against the willow
and snatches it back — the bark is white with heat,
with fever. The impression left by her palm
boils over with sap, amber-voiced,
high-pitched, thick: *This*
is where the soul goes
when it has cut the cloud's throat,
where it rains and roots and breathes

itself into bark, needle and leaf, this
is where it blisters and withers. The yew
went to sleep in a gas oven, the willow
went to sleep in a stream. Pansies
and rosemary, thought and memory. The yew
knew her shadow and soon
she will give birth. The grey earth
bulges around the roots of the yew.
Agriope kneels at the tree's pelvis and stares
and the earth bulges again and ruptures
and a blunt nose thrusts out from the hole,
its nostrils rippling with panic, and Agriope
digs until her fingers are raw and she can clasp
the infant at the back of its skull
and feel it struggling underground,
its muscles tense as saplings bent back in a bow,
and she throws her weight and tugs and the infant
is the arrow, thin and wooden it surges forward
from the archer, the earth, the face comes
unfleshed, a calcium moon,
the blind eyes red as yew berries,
the bone-hard shoulders come,
the hoar frost mane,
the bone-hard torso comes,
the Christ-cradle rib cage, those scaffolds of snow,
the front hooves, flint arrowheads,
thrash and lacerate its mother's roots,
and the yew clutches at its child,
but the child
kicks free.
And emerges entangled

in the sun's black hair: the albino mare,

Ariel. And the mare, salty and bleached

with the sweat of its birth, bites through

the umbilicus.

A draft through the branches,

mercury-cool: *Use*

this horse to ford the arroyo, but

after the fording, you must

let her go.

Sonnets to Orpheus 1.3

She goes to the oracle, she goes inside the temple of stone
where everything has stopped, except the ants panicking
across the oracle's face, the face pale and hard from the
waters of the Hebros, the mouth open, the lips cracked.
She stands before the oracle and sings a prayer, and as she
sings she watches his closed eyes, his open mouth. She
sings a prayer, she asks for water and the oracle does not
answer. She sees where the blood has stopped in his throat.
She sees where the wind has died into his lips and mouth,
where wind has become stone, where stone holds the
breath of water and wind is a song that no wind is singing,
and she stops her prayer. The ants go across the oracle's
lips, they go inside his mouth, they come out of his mouth.
She swallows, and watches the ants, and knows they mean
nothing. They go across his lips, they go inside his mouth,
they come out of his mouth.

She knows he would not ask for tears, she knows he does
not need them, she knows the ants mean nothing and
knows her tears mean nothing here. The salt in her throat.
And she cannot stop. She cannot get the song out of her
body. The ants go across the oracle's lips, they go inside his
mouth. She touches the oracle's lips with her lips, and goes
out of the temple.

The Dead Water

Handprints of rain in her lap.*

---

* ORPHEUS:

All winter we listened
for the rain, listened
for the catch in the throat
of the crocus, for the oaks
to open their small uncountable
mouths and exhale their living jades.

I listened for your dolphin
laughter. Your breath. Your pulse,
ultraviolet. The sound of rain
on the soundboard of your window. The white
horizon of your wrist.

*

Autumn breathes its red breath
on the windows of the earth;
rain meditates on Thetis Lake.

*

The handless clock trying to hold
the hour of death, salt
in the last mouthful of water.
The windows opaque with silence,
silence stagnating in the wineglass.

2

The night you called the rain
through the open window
with your hands, I wanted to hold
your playing in a wineglass of words, to say
your hands. Your hands
had made themselves manifest,
I said words and walked out
into the speechless streets.

*

Sitting with you in Arbutus Cove.
Death, and an undone button
on your blue shirt. Your fingers
drumming the rhythm of your reading
into the driftwood between us.

*

50

That day in the rain you showed me
the sheet music for Lorca's poem,
read his letter. The breath
of birds trying to stitch a tear
in space, the notes on the sheet
coming unhitched. We left
light shadows on the wet bench.

3

I wanted to give you something
you could hold in the hour
when the oak leaves are a sieve.

I gave you the hand of autumn,
the broken glass from its lung.
Paper-white petals in a white paper
envelope; nothing more than words
pencilled between blue lines.

*

What I wanted: water
already dead, the last breath,
held, the huge blue fermata,
and the corpse evaporating
from the crocus-golden hill.

*

I wanted to give you
silence, space
between finger and key,
hammer and string. The open
hand. The bone
of sound inside
the rain.

Tennessee Waltz

Agriope wears a hay-coloured cotton dress and an abalone
bracelet. The summer has scattered freckles on her cheeks.
She clasps Orpheus's hand as she would a dragonfly,
carefully. They walk together across the grass toward the
gazebo. The scent of cut lilacs and goldenrod is strong, the
sunlight is white Italian wine. She feels her heart, the arm
of her heart in her arm, the hand of her heart in his hand,
his fingers fine as the branches of a dragonfly's wing.

They are dancing when she notices Persephone, alone at a
table in the corner. Persephone stands and her names fall
like scarves, evening, twilight, night. Agriope steps back;
Persephone flows into Orpheus's arms. The salt of her body,
her gleaming mineral thinking, marks his skin. The song is
in geologic time.

Agriope sits in Persephone's chair, her friend's long
red gloves wrinkled like snakeskins on the table. She
contemplates the empty wine glass, the red aureole where
the bowl meets the stem, the semicircle where Persephone's
lips met the lip of the glass, and a wasp, like the point of
a compass, circling the rim. Agriope glances up, spots the
hive. The waltz ends; the bracelet — cracks.

Narcissus

Her footprint pooling with blue.*

---

* ORPHEUS:

A gypsy moth panicking between

the Fleuve Saint-Laurent

and the Mare Imbrium,

the map of Montréal

and the map of the moon.

I wake in my basement apartment

amongst the roots of water,

the splintering of pipes,

the faucets wailing upstairs,

the ache and creak of ocean

under the maps on the walls,

dry narcissus petals shored

against the baseboards,

Lorca's "Narciso" drying

over the back of a chair.   53

This morning I read your letter,

the twine untwined and the silk

wrinkled like the skin of a slate-

blue snake, its bones unfolded

on the table. I read your fragile

inventory: two slices of orange,

one plum pit, the small cup

with its blue fish, the vein

of orange paint at your wrist.

After your hands,
I have held many things.
Last night I held the paintbrush
but it was a stiff minnow of maple,
and I tasted the sable
that your tongue had tasted,
but it was dull blue with dried paint.

Last night I could not sleep
and your scrape at my door
made me stumble in the dark for a match,
and I knocked the glass of water,
soaking the matchbook and soaking the poem.

Now I want to cut my tongue on the brush
and I want to cut the stream in your palm.

The old panic, the old ache
in my palms. But your flesh
reflects my flesh. The map
of your left foot, the gash
of the Gulf of California,
aims itself west, towards the shadows
of leaves swimming across the threshold,
and further west, where the Pacific
convalesces in the harbour.

Fragment 36

P,

Herakleitos says, *Water's death generates earth.* Red leaves
falling through the lead bars on the window, igniting the floor.
Ants sparking around a honeyed spoon, a smashed cup, bones
of bone china shining around the ants. I have not touched the
piano since I met Orpheus. Last night, a blackout in this hall,
built from stone in 1913, choked by the quartz-barked climbing
vines. I am writing to ask about petrifaction.

He argued. His axiom is many and mine is one. I need not to
need him. He said a word and the world contracted like an iris
around it: *her.* My body does not argue. But it burns. I heard my
voice arguing with itself, arguing about a fever which he has
never felt, I felt the rain throbbing hotter at my throat and wrist.
He kissed me, quickly — wind skinning stone.

This afternoon I woke and couldn't move. The sky bruised my
eyes with rain's weight and my body was a held breath. My
nerves tore through his fingerprints, stripped themselves like
copper wire, stretched into the room and scraped against things,
a notebook, a thread, *the ragged edge of a letter* — every thing
ten thousand amps.

And this evening my nerves flick electricity into the sheets. I force
myself to the bathroom where I bathe the nerves burning at my
wrist, the tap water hits them and turns to steam. In the mirror, I
see the glint of silica on my lips. My ghost goes for refuge in the
sarcophagus of my skull. The body does not argue.

Last night, a blackout in this hall. He is here with me. He touches fast, thirst in his fingers. His saliva scalding my throat, my shoulder. There is never enough time. He turns away from me and I move my hand over his side, slow, thinking hard about what I am touching, how I love each rib and the breath bending each rib. These bone ribs and the lead ribs on the window, his flesh and the smooth stone wall, his saliva and the hatred of rain. The rain cooling to the temperature of the lead. The world becoming one.

The piano, lockjawed. The violin scarved in silks, its case shoved under my bed. I can hear the slack strings slackening, the wood hardening in the humid dark. Every day I wake inside the knowledge that I am wrong, and that knowledge is the geology of this body, its fossils of frayed copper wire.

Herakleitos says, *Out of earth originates water.* My friend, you know: is he lying?

A

Basalt

A snapdragon gnashing against her hand.*

---

* ORPHEUS:
I stared at the intricate
stitched leather of your boot,
the hem of your burgundy skirt,
your lips, the way they tensed against
words as if they were figs.

I came to your room in a blackout,
electricity wilted in the clocks,
your clothes drying over cupboard doors.
I gave you a mandarin orange
from the market in Chinatown.

You remembered a naked childhood,
southern suns constellating themselves
into your flesh. The freckles on the knuckles
of your left hand were the extremity of a sky
I had never seen, though I saw wrist, forearm,
the naked lines of your hand drawing
those of your shoulder, your throat.

You gave me a piece of Spanish basalt,
said, This is a worry stone, you worry it
with your thumb. I asked, Have you
worried it? You slipped the stone
into your mouth, and soothed it.

You undressed the mandarin,

shared with me its many rays,

your radiant fingers, your hand

that had played in the rapids

of the piano, that had held

mandarin, snapdragon,

the gasp of basalt,

my hand.

Abalone

A,

This stone is for holding down this note, this stone is for
returning to the side of the road where I found it, where I stood
in the fluorescent light of a telephone booth on an ocean road
and stared at this stone while on the line you sang a song about
turquoise. I wanted this note to be quiet, quiet as turquoise,
fluorescence, surf, quiet as the bracelet you left on my pillow,
the cracked abalone bracelet that you removed from the music
of many bracelets at your wrist.

But as you said: I am not quiet. I have slept for seven months
— I am no less sharp for having done so. Anger is a galaxy, black
milk and flint stars. Your silence wounds me as light wounds the
blind earth; I try to turn away from it but it is everywhere.

The light from those days was grass light, light of the fragile
June grasses that grew on Beacon Hill. We leaned against our
fallen bicycles and the day thinned into a thousand, thousand
stalks of light. It was grass light, reed light, light of whisky-
soaked harmonica reed, aster and acorn and abalone light.
Every day was lit with that light.

I met you under an oak tree, you were biting blackberry thorns
from your thumbs. You had a violin with abalone tuning keys,
you had that stolen harmonica in a minor key, and while
you played piano, the silver bracelets shivered on your bare
forearms. You showed me where the blackberries were,

and we sat in your car, rain on the windscreen, eating
handfuls of blackberries and drinking whisky from your flask.
I followed you to the bent tree in the bay, we did not speak
and the beach was a stretch of darkness and pale shells, a
chart of stars, and wind in the rigging of the anchored ships.

Silence is an ear-shaped shell, sea-ear, ormer, mother-of-pearl.

The night of the Leonid meteor storm at Maltby Lake, I lost
the mopalia shell, the one the seagull gave me and I kept
in my pocket, it was the mossy colour of rusted copper, a
carapace of rain. You sat across from me at the bonfire. The
Hyades came unfixed. A turquoise star tore the sky in half.

The taste of harmonica, cobwebs and blackberries. The
evening tuned with abalone. You were already married to
the rain.

The last time I saw you, you were a silhouette in your ochre
chair by the window, your boots up and braced against the
frame. You ashed your cigarette into the window box and
sang, and when it was time for me to go, you walked with me
to the ocean. It was so still, not even the murmur of surf, only
the long, pearl-grey twilight of water.

No, sorrow is not an ear-shaped shell, a silent violin. Not an
abalone bracelet. Not a roadside stone.

O

Metamorphoses, Book 10

When Agriope plays piano, the shades
listen, the poplar and the willow are still
with listening, a single hawk
nails itself against the wind.
The light staggers three times
through the house of Pisces,
the geology of Haides' city
dances in a rigid grid. She is
stiff-fingered, her grief
is small as a salamander's
hand, her hair is long
as the rain's.
Every tree in the grove,
an interval of silence.
The ivory gate,
open. Echoing.

The Deep Song of Persephone

She strokes two notes from the tamboura, cold pulse under
the roads of song, moulted knives in every alley and verse,
fossils of wind in her throat, dance of sand shaped by wind,
thin filaments of basaltic glass, knives of crows caress
her breast, whet themselves on her jawbone, her cheeks,
the flesh-red feldspar of her lips, which tense themselves
around her silence, sap of pearwood and sycamore, sap of
seven garnets, seven pomegranate seeds, she strokes two
notes from the tamboura and lava rises in the throat of
night, dissolves the fossils of black wind, dissolves the body
of the one who listens, but what lacks a voice cannot call
lapilli from the eyes of night, cannot call salt and water from
stone, no no no no no no no stone cannot call water from
stone.

Border

Rain scattered like samara through the grass.*

---

* ORPHEUS:

In the dry lands,
rain is not rain.

It is a noise
that wakes me
long before dawn.

The persephone-faced
crow at the window,
whispering my name.

The deaths I died
in that country
were as wide as a day.
They happened in my hands
holding the many letters
that were not your body.

I never learned to live
as the river lives,
my body shedding itself
to become a windpipe of clay,
a larynx of gravel and rushes,
breathing the leaves
that children lent me.

But I can say that death
is a summer,
and the maple tree
never turns yellow.

And now I have nothing
to give you:
the small olives
of my sweat
in a deerskin pouch;
dandelion ash, acorns
and maple keys;
my mouth and hands
cracked with dryness.

I have not brought
the seeds of rain
I promised to bring
in the palm of my hand,
the water that gathers
on the canvas of a tent
after a night of breathing.

64

Unsent Letter

All summer the Don River had been choked to a khaki creek, and I had been reading Simone Weil, and my thinking had been like the river's, pinched, turbid, lethargic. I would cross the viaduct on my way to the library; at night, through the veil, I could see campfires flickering like pennies in the valley.

In her New York notebook, Weil writes: *Water, image of attentiveness. The matter which resembles nothingness.*

I had two rocks, gifts from an effulgent Italian, smuggled out from under the oracle at Delphi. The culture's wisdom was inscribed in the stone there. On the one hand, *Know yourself*; and on the other, *Nothing excessive.* The virtues of Greece, a knife gripped in its sheath. The rocks were cold with a solar coldness.

After the smog broke, I did most of my reading on the balcony. Wasps, the whine of brass prayer bowls, the aroma of sunflowers from the morning coffee. In the window box, the basil was a big gasp of chlorophyll, a gnomon, a green calmness, a Doric column of self-knowing, deep with patience.

In the sprawling monologue by the Italian cosmologist, Plato describes time as a mobile image of eternity. Weil describes imbalance as a mobile image of balance, the oscillating strife as phenomena crawl from the infinite and fall back into it, *according to natural law: for they inflict justice and retaliative tax upon one another for injustice according to Khronos's tactics.* Revenge is ever excessive. True justice is hydrostatic, exemplified by water, the matrix, with its ensemble of little levers, which stills itself into equilibrium.

There is a prayer that was found inscribed on gold foil and enclosed in a talisman in Italy. It warns of the spring of forgetfulness, watched by a white cypress; it says to wait for the lake of recollection. Weil asserts that when one is sick with thirst, the thought of water is a cry with one's whole soul. Orpheus saw a swan's reflection, drank from the wrong well. His neck curved like a bass clef, like a long narcosis. Wear the prayer close to your skin.

At the end of summer, in the middle of a storm, I placed the Delphic rocks in a metal bowl on the balcony. I was near the library when the sky cleared, I remember the rusted eaves of a house with a half-open door where someone was practising the piano, a single, circular earring on the damp pavement. I walked home across the viaduct, there were fire trucks parked on the road, a frost-white, one-eyed dog, I glanced over the edge and the Don River was flooded, the floodwater nursing itself on emergency lights and moon, the entire valley: a moving image of eternity.

At home, the bowl had overflowed. I recall the taste of the water: nickel, and earth, and nothingness.

A

Georgics, Book 4

Aristaios paddled out to the cove
where Teiresias took his siesta
and he beached the canoe
on the jaundiced rocks and walked
among the lazing seals to the place
where the snake was drunk on sun and wind,
and Aristaios snatched him by the throat.
Teiresias thrashed and turned
into tide pool, left his skin in the fist
of Aristaios, who smashed his free hand
into the water where the snake
had disappeared. Up to his elbow
in brine, Aristaios saw himself
grasping himself from below, saw
his arm grown into the arm
of another, and he tore his wrist out
of his twin in the water. His reflection
would not rest and Teiresias had shed
the wind like hawk-skin, like a sheath
of feathers, and had turned into
Aristaios. Aristaios
sat back on the rocks and stared at the wind
and the sun on the water, ran the dry snakeskin
through his damp hands, wind in the wings
of kelp, and asked himself why it would not rain.
And the water would not sleep against
the rocks and the wind would not forgive

the water and the seals groaned and woke
and went back to the sea. Aristaios drank
a hard yellow liquor and the sun
sank, leaving heat in his chest.
Then the snake came.
It scraped its fresh scales against
his calf and scraped its sharpened jaw
against his ankle, it stroked him
the way the swords of water stroke
the shore, but the snake
would not speak.
Aristaios let the snakeskin
drop and spat the warmth
out of his mouth.

Leontion, Book 3

HERMESIANAX: The story is wrong. Sitting here in the
stark light of ten years later, it is hard to believe what I saw.
But the taboo against looking back was grafted to the truth.
Those Roman storytellers adore laws, they love covenants
witnessed by the river Styx, the logos uttered by the current,
its xylophone of stones. Haides said go if you haven't had
a pomegranate, go, but don't look back. The Styx listened.
(Seven red stars, a week without rain, the constellation of
the ox.) But that story is wrong.

When I first saw her, she was glowing in the light of a
poem, she was walking at Willows Beach, and beneath her
feet the sand was turning to glass. The music of a trailing
mosaic. The moon showing its bone-china face in each
mirror. It was, truly, the work of excruciation. But what is
more difficult: to endure gravity after the magnet dies, the
relentless silence after the god lets you drop from its jaws:
to continue being human.

In that ugly and stubborn place, the lawless Kokytos wails
in its straitjacket of reeds; the three-headed dog sharpens
his bark in fire, in fire hardens his eye. What I want is just
the structure, the katabatic arc. There is a wild-eyed one,
daughter of water; there is a lake of ice. "Agriope" is a more
ancient name for Eurydike. It was she who entered the
grove, who went down to the water, looking, looking for her
friend, Persephone. These two: I set them in the catalogue

beside madness-fettered Pythagoras, with his delicate helix, his heaven-mirroring sphere; and Sokrates, escaped from the love-kiln, who knew no cure, and so curled into the quarrelling maze.

It is spring; calypso orchids cry out to the mountains. It is autumn; two autumns. It is spring; the artificial light falls on the borrowed rosewood desk, its dolphin-call sonographs, its horse-nostril whorls. The mercury, a broken and furious demon, burns in its little glass cell. For years I have injured my eyes with words. I now own too many papers, more than I can carry on my back. But sometimes, rarely, I am permitted a glimpse of her: she flashes across someone's face, grass catches fire just under the surface of the stream. There is one thing that I know: they were wrong, the Pythagoreans and the Orphics, what they thought was blasphemy: the body is not a tomb. No — it is a temple! The body is a temple. And the light that passes through it is wild, the light is the world's.

Let me go once more down to the water. Not the forgetting water, but the one of witnessing. Let the moon follow me on its long heron legs. Or let the moon be a swan.

I was there, I saw: they emerged from the earth, the two of them, together, lurching, it is true, like an awkward thaw, but they were together, I swear.

Nautical Astrology

Aristotle says Thales says *thalassa*
is the archaic origin of all things.

In the temple of Apollo,
Thales is scratching in the sand
with a hollow fennel stalk.
On the altar is the cup,
his offering to the god.
He is composing his nautical
astrology, about the sun's turns
and equal days. He writes,
The earth, like a ship,
rests on water. Watch
the stars of Arktouros
to steer your way home.
His mind, the night sky's
mobile, submerged to the waist
in the bottom of a well.

Aristotle says Thales says all things
are full of gods. When Agriope enters,
the floor has been swept,
and Thales immersed in silence
that the light cancels out.
But the cup, a plenum, a pantheon;
the water, umbrous, most wise.
Agriope drinks the dark sacrament
of Okeanos.

THE SAME RIVER

Another common description in the Roman period was 'the weeping philosopher'. This latter judgement is entirely trivial, being founded partly on humorous references to the idea that all things flow like rivers ...

— KIRK, RAVEN & SCHOFIELD

Euphorbia lactea, **Allan Gardens**

This cactus, dry and cranky
as the mind of Herakleitos,
a many-tentacled tidal wave
arrested mid-crash and still
crashing, the gnarled arthritic
rivers of time, photographed
from eternity. The soul,
pale as cactus sap, tries
to stand upright, a column
of light, but gravity,
gorgon-haired, lizard-skinned,
shaper of parabolas, harmony's
architect, turns it back
to the tonic of its roots.

No: not the Rossetti wrist
of the violinist, but a bouquet
of crossbows, a weeping
tree of scorpion tails;
analysis, arson's logic,
styled with mortality;
the fever-struck body, seizuring
arch-backed on the hard bunk.
It is one form, one kind
of wisdom, disciplined by fire.

The Eight Hypotheses:
Parmenides vs. Herakleitos

PARMENIDES: I feel like the old race-horse in [Ibykos's poem], who trembles at the start of the chariot-race ... finding himself, so late in life, forced into the lists of love.

— PLATO

All [Plato's characteristic] graces and mollifications are lacking in the second part of our dialogue [Parmenides], *and those critics who find in it an exhibition of rollicking fun must possess an enviable sense of humour.*

— FRANCIS MACDONALD CORNFORD

1 (Starring Parmenides as himself)

Parmenides drove in the long red Dodge
through the gate of day, the axle
blazing in the naves, the bronze
gateposts blazing in their sockets.
The blonde in the bikini
behind the wheel said, If the day
had a shape it would be
a sphere. She snapped down the sun visor
and stepped on the accelerator.
If the day had a body it would be
limited and indivisible, she said,
and rolled down the window and spat

a hydrogen atom at the speeding road.
The single seed of aetherial fire
that sprouts the dialectical tree.

Herakleitos, hitching, caught the atom
in his palm, made a fist
and breathed into it, forging
water.

2 (Starring Parmenides as Pamela the lifeguard)

And there was Herakleitos, both feet
in that myth of persistence, the river.
The water is unreal, said Parmenides,
the river is one of the names you have
for the one, which is unnamed
and the same with itself, unlike
the water which changes under the name
of the river. Horseshit, said Herakleitos,
kicking the river in Parmenides' face.
So what, said Parmenides, the water,
though false, is also the one, and blew
his pink whistle.

3 (Starring Parmenides as Jacques Lacan's analysand)

I dreamt I was in a grocery store,
said Parmenides, I had a spherical
shopping basket labelled ESTI
and I was galloping down the aisles
frantically cramming everything
into the basket, all the cans of kidney
and garbanzo beans, all the tacos,
every frigging pepper, red, yellow,
jalapeño, you name it, and when
I was finished, the store was empty, and you
were the cashier. Your fifty minutes is terminated,
said Herakleitos, igniting his cigar. Fire,
he added, is like hard cash: the signifier
signifying everything.

4 (Starring Parmenides as Herakleitos)

And there was Herakleitos, both feet
in that repeating myth, the river.
Parmenides was right, he said, what exists
is fixed, it's the same river from last time.
His disciple, Kratylos, lifted a crayfish
and fingered it skeptically. Then he
frowned, and pointed as the wet flux
became the Phlegethon, the river
of fire. Those are sharp little triangles,
said Herakleitos as the fire divided
and cut his Achilles tendon. Yes,
those are fast and philosophical piranhas,
said Herakleitos — and was instantly

77

incinerated. Kratylos
freed the crayfish, which had become
an organ pipe cactus.

5 (Starring Parmenides as the Miltonic voice)

Of Man's First Disobedience, and the Fruit
Of that Forbidden Tree, began Parmenides'
disembodied monologue in a monochrome void —
Hey, said Herakleitos tanning under a sunlamp,
have you tried a certain Cox's Orange Pippin?
It tastes like sex, death, infrared, yellow
jackets, dandelion spears and nut-brown
beer.

6 (Starring Parmenides as James Joyce)

Squinting out of his cyclopean eye,
Parmenides wrote: The inaudible totality
of snow, descending on the somnambulant
mortals and immortals. The street lamp held them
in its tent of phosphorescence. You need sleep,
prescribed Herakleitos, you ain't slept
and you've gone psycho, like an extra
from *Night of the Living Dead.*

7 (Starring Parmenides as Orson Welles in *The Third Man*)

At the zenith of the Ferris wheel,
Parmenides pointed at the people below:
I deny the dyad, he said, they don't
understand their unreality. We are
nearer to the sun, said Herakleitos,
the radius of the Ferris wheel
is within the radius of the flame,
the heat you feel on your face
is the heat they feel on theirs,
you cannot contain its life, combusting
while symmetrically snuffing out,
but the circumference of day is cut
by the diameter of night. Fuck
the diameter, said Parmenides,
I have floodlights.

8 (Starring Parmenides as the Author Function)

On the second floor of Carberry Gardens,
Parmenides was typing while the sun
was rising. The day was many shades
of blue, so Parmenides imagined
greyness: a geometrical solid, shaped
like a sphere, bloated with homogeneous
being. A letter from Herakleitos
rested beside the keyboard, irregular.
Dear Herakleitos, I miss the strength
of your mind, he typed,

(Fragment)

I miss the sanity
of your hands. In my dreams you walk weeping along
the Otonabee River, it is winter, you are hitching the wild
highway between Peterborough and Moosonee.

I remember your burnt matches curling, the innumerable
arguments, calamari and cold tea at the Chinese restaurant,
perogies and beer at The Grapefruit Moon.

I remember the depth of your sleep on St. Stephen's Day,
leaving you at dawn in the arms of that woman, and walking
home in the ash-white and holy light.

Potato

Soul of Phaidros! Dumb
dirt-smudged earnest
to learn. Eyed
like Argos, a peacock's
sepia-toned tail.
Beauty stampedes
your pupils,
irrigates the stumps
of your wings,
and suddenly
you're bristling
with little penises.
No longer a dull
meteorite
but quilled
with light,
ready for the Indy 500
on the ridge of heaven.
Terrestrial apple, angelic
tuber. Ordinary
Ontario table potato,
cause of cicada song
and Sokratic madness,
spunky as those arachnid
Aristophanic spheres —
cut in half, you reflect
the translucent, trillium-
white heart
of your other self.

The Day

SOKRATES: [What if an idea] were like one and the same day,
which is in many places at the same time and nevertheless is
not separate from itself ...
— PLATO

The spring light is
palinodic. All that I've done,
I want to take back. The old
Eleatic master seems to think
the problem of participation
is about the just distribution
of stuff. But what if
an idea can't be
cut up and passed out
like a canvas sail? The day
is an idea and each thing
is thinking it, iridescently,
and each thought is a spoke
in the solar wheel. But this
crocus is also its own idea
of whiteness, the only dissent
in a consensus of purple.
The idea dies with it — but
that doesn't mean it can't be
known, an odour like coldness
from a garden hose, the song
of city water transposed

for the piccolo, a profile
distinct as a six-eared star.

   At a sidewalk market,
the autumn spectrum
of apples: the sunset
has condensed in them.
It's beauty's accusation:
if you live your entire life over —
you'll never be equal to it.
I stand there at the corner, known
by the equinox and knowing
nothing, exposed by the alethic
light of those apples,
that fearless crocus,
the magnolia tree, its chandelier
of tears.

HAREY'S PRAYERS

It has been described as a symphony in geometry, but we lack the ears to hear it.

— STANISŁAW LEM

Red Sun

Inside that silver ellipsoid it is raining.
Like a young fern, like a foetus curled
around the umbilicus, he is curled
around his little pain. The ascesis
climbs him in flickering insectile
tides, and the rain, your rain,
pins his extremities to the bed
with exquisite sterling pins,
and in every pin is an army
of six-limbed seraphim, and in the hand
of every seraph is a flail forged
from rain, your rain, and they are threshing
his soul like a fern, like a fist
of wheat that refuses to give up
its desiccated grains.
                    And like the rain, and like you,
I am indifferent to his suffering.
He did not love me while I lived;
why should he mourn my second
death? If you are forgetfulness,
recall your infantry —
visit him yourself.

Blue Sun

Let me sacrifice my desire to you. Why
did you let me have thirst,
why hearing, if you intended
to be salt, eternally,
and silent? Unlike
quietudes shared by humans,
your silence has no meaning:
it is a weed, vascular as light,
driving its rhizomes deep
into my hearing. It is sheer
metre, not order but gross
regularity, two figures repeating
in infinite regress, trough and crest.
It is the very inverse of prayer,
species of emptied listening,
a sparrow, apparently, here,
but sparred with void.
Sometimes music is most like
a flock of birds in flight, every muscle
flexing in sympathy — meanwhile
you legislate your sexless
gravity.
           You are not erotic. The slow bolero
of your body exhausts itself on the rocks.
I kneel on your shore but I do not
believe in you and I do not
offer my prayer to you; let me sacrifice
my desire on your altar of false
water.

Red Sun

You do not remember
the names of the drowned, you are
the negative of memory, let me
remind you: my heart, its red
antlers, the day you made
the birds, they were faceless,
shapeless, a parody of music,
they moved over the face
of the waters, you separated
the sun from itself, the azure
from the infrared, my heart
was chambered, branching, arctic
light clenched my lungs, I was
climaxing between isn't
and is, the intravenous scar
flared on my arm, an auricle
of light, I was listening
to the birds as they moved
upon the abyss, spermatozoa,
syllables in a dead language
articulating death, my heart,
its red antlers, tangled
in his foliate grief.
            And having made
the birds, you damned them.

Blue Sun

You are not a god, though you are hostile
as a god, inhospitable and anonymous
as a metropolis, your grey and single-
minded industry transforming the shore
into yourself. Narcissism is not
self-love, but a mechanism of survival,
your cogs churning amorphous as maggots,
pallid as almonds, paper-whites, the high
notes of foam. Your self is a cosmetic
fiction, a centrifuge. Vainglorious,
despotic as the gods of the old books,
their brittle, dendritic hierarchies,
their rage for stasis,
you assimilate all that you touch
to the empire of the undifferentiated.
I kneel here, where you limn my world,
where my world lessens into you,
phantasmagoric, fluid, pristine
machine, forceful
as pornography, inverse
image of poverty,
and though my desires
siphon to the finest
point, I cannot fathom
how you appear
to be and are
not.

Red Sun

I take aim at the cloud, I stand

inside the libraries of rain, arcane

codes, columns, Corinthian

columns of storm, the more Roman,

ornamental, the more criminal

the columns, the regal, hydrogen-

beaded spines, coronating in a knuckled

bunch of nerves and bugling out in tongue,

cankered with language, glossolalic,

greedy, colonizing silence,

converting it. I take aim

at the cloud and my want

is a dart, a dark error,

its vaned tail shivering

in vespers' grip, but

there is some rust on me

called sin, called self,

colour of cinnamon, saffron,

of the moss where my want lay down

and was lost. I stand

inside the libraries, oracles

of storm, and I raise

my auto-barked arm and take aim

at the cloud, the rain carving

me out of darkness, the spike of blood

thudding in my temple, the little horses

digging their hooves into my wrist,

their manes braided with your ninety-
nine Arabic names, I take aim,
but the dart, like a limp compass needle,
has gone dead in my hand.

Blue Sun

Let me praise you, as you prefer,

by denying all that you are not:

not the cherry blossoming

in November, the blossoms

in the gutter, not the wrongness

or the gorgeousness of that,

not the night we bent down

the cherry boughs and drank

rain's acrid nectar,

not the afternoon I slept

on the hill and he found me

there, my mind in its oval

of bone and the bone in the bronze

alcove of grass and my body going on

in the infinite dream of the field,

not the field, not spring in the field,

everything straining to praise

you, not the sky's sapphire confession,

not the crocus with its curved

blue hurt, not the garish fires

of the daffodils, and not the grass,

not this stalk of grass, long

and slendered by longing, singular,

given over to the invisible and the ideal

of the geometrical line, but too gentle,

the feather of its thought too textured

and too gentle,

　　　　　　　not geometry,

discipline of proportion, reciprocity,

not the roots, the branches, the brief

flush of blossoms, not the fractals

of justice, not the father

of rain manifest

out of the whirlwind

to repudiate my prayer.

RAIN SUTRA

*

The rain is Art Blakey
with the arms of Indra,
the ten thousand things
banging down on the shingles.
In the morning, the flowering crab
is fragile and indigent
and black, limbs strict
as lightning.
The spider's pattern is
irreparable. And yet, an arpeggio
on your piano, the sutra of water
suggesting the web.

*

The Texas sky is starless:
your piano, silent. This
is the song he sings
to you and you
are singing it. The tune
is a circumference
of light, and your voice
the difference between you
and the nickel-strung
darkness. The desert sand
lays down a bass line, pulsed
with your footprints,
bleached like a text
by Georgia O'Keeffe.
The stone in your hand,
black as a semitone
set in the key of evening.

*

The wind is finger-picking
the first bars in the grass;
listening, you let the scarf
of your voice follow its lead.
Against the bronze and yellow
field, indigo, drifting;
listening, you let fall
three glass beads, the three
syllables in the nightingale's
name. Almost night, not
raining; but a listless pealing,
tintinnating like rain.

*

Pennies, flat and effaced, sparks

thrown off by the sun,

hot copper ellipses cooling

as night rises, now,

from the hood of your car.

A couple of fireflies, the sporadic

ticking of the rad.

Your voice, an evening

in late June, ice losing

its edges in a jar of tea.

*

I want to be

in Texas, asleep

in the passenger seat of your

nineteen seventy-two sky-blue

Cadillac, the windscreen hypnotized

by horizon, the rear-view

by your eyes, their roan-brown

focus, the careless

freckles on your cheeks,

the breeze sight-reading

a scarred bass clef,

your left hand in your curls,

your bare foot on the gas,

your skin resonant

with fading light, Nina Simone

on the radio and the rain

starting warm on my arm, the way

you play piano, scattering

a handful of dice

on a wood surface,

every note, one side

of five silences.

*

You wake in white
sheets in a New York
morning, the descending snow
elegant as a Duke Ellington
solo, the sun auditing
each note exactly. You
extend your hand, the beige
cadence of your arm, find
the warmth where his body
was. From the kitchen,
that familiar resonance,
tap water striking teakettle.

Notes

¶ Epigraph: Federico García Lorca, "From a letter to Melchor Fernández Almagro, July/August 1922," *A Season in Granada: Uncollected Poems and Prose*, trans. and ed. Christopher Maurer (London: Anvil Press Poetry, 1998), p. 55.

OFELIA: ¶ Epigraph: Stefania Kozakowska, "Young Poland: 'Genius Artists,' Neo-Romantics and Decadents," *Between Two Worlds: The Art of Poland 1890-1914* (National Museum in Cracow / Vancouver Art Gallery, ca. 2000), p. 13.

THE UNCOLLECTED WORKS OF SALLIE CHISUM: ¶ Epigraph: Michael Ondaatje, *Coming Through Slaughter* (Concord: House of Anansi Press, 1976), p. 78.

THE METAMORPHOSIS OF AGRIOPE: ¶ Epigraph: Rainer Maria Rilke, "Orpheus. Eurydice. Hermes," *The Poetry of Rilke*, trans. Edward Snow (New York: North Point Press, 2009), p. 203. ¶ "Unsent Letter": "Water, image of attentiveness...." Simone Weil, *La connaissance surnaturelle* (Paris: Gallimard, 1950), p. 57. ¶ "... according to natural law ..." Anaximandros, Diels-Kranz 12A9.

THE SAME RIVER: ¶ Epigraph: G.S. Kirk, J.E. Raven & M. Schofield, *The Presocratic Philosophers*, 2nd ed. (Cambridge: Cambridge University Press, 1983), p. 183. ¶ "The Eight Hypotheses": Epigraph 1: Plato, *Parmenides* 136e-137a, trans. F.M. Cornford. ¶ Epigraph 2: Francis MacDonald Cornford, *Plato and Parmenides* (London: Routledge & Kegan Paul Ltd, 1951), p. 114. ¶ "The Day": Epigraph: Plato, *Parmenides* 131b, trans. F.M. Cornford.

HAREY'S PRAYERS: ¶ Epigraph: Stanisław Lem, *Solaris*, trans. Joanna Kilmartin and Steve Cox (London: Faber and Faber, 1970), p. 126.

Cast of Characters

Most of the poems in this book are spoken through masks.
(Transliterations of Greek names, rather than their standard
Romanizations, have been used throughout the text.)

AGRIOPE
Another, older name for Eurydike.

ARISTAIOS
A Greek pastoral god. In one story, he learns from Proteus, the
shape-changing old man of the sea, that his bees have perished as
punishment for the death of Eurydike, who was bitten by a snake
while fleeing him.

ART BLAKEY
An American drummer and bandleader.

VAN DEN BUDENMAYER
A Dutch composer, imagined by the Polish composer Zbigniew
Preisner and director Krzysztof Kieślowski.

SALLIE CHISUM
A relative of John Chisum, the cattle baron whose faction made use
of Billy the Kid in the Lincoln County War. Billy the Kid was shot and
killed at the conclusion of that war by Pat Garrett, whom Chisum
had helped to elect as sheriff. (Cf. Michael Ondaatje, *The Collected
Works of Billy the Kid.*)

DUKE ELLINGTON
An American jazz pianist, composer and bandleader.

HAREY (or Hari or Rheya)
A character in Andrei Tarkovsky's film *Solaris*. In Lem's book of
the same title, there are two suns, a red one and a blue one. Harey
is married to the cosmonaut Kelvin, commits suicide, and is
resurrected by a sentient ocean.

HERAKLEITOS of Ephesos
A Greek philosopher, unfairly caricatured as a proponent of the
extreme doctrine that all things flow (cf. Plato, *Kratylos* 402a;

Simplikios, Commentary on Aristotle's *Physics* 1313.11). Herakleitos himself insists, "Listening not to me but to the Logos it is wise to agree that all things are one" (Diels-Kranz 22B50, trans. Kirk, Raven & Schofield). Unlike some other monists, he is acutely sensitive to the tension between the one and the many, which he calls a "back-turned attunement," and exemplifies with the bow and the lyre. (Cf. esp. Charles H. Kahn, *The Art and Thought of Heraclitus*.)

HERMESIANAX of Kolophon
A Hellenistic elegist. His three-book poem, named after his lover, includes his testimony to Agriope's return from the underworld.

INDRA
A Hindu god of war and storm.

OFELIA of Fitzroy Road
Not Hamlet's echo.

GEORGIA O'KEEFFE
An American painter.

PARMENIDES of Elea
A Greek philosopher, called the "antinaturalist" by Aristotle (cf. Sextus Empiricus, *Against the Physicists* 2.46). The first part of his poem — a hybrid of logic and apocalypse — attempts to deduce the true nature of being from the premise "it is," and is driven to infer that mortal faith in the diversity of shifting things must be mistaken. (*Esti* is the third person singular, present indicative of the Greek verb *einai*, "to be": "is.") The second part of his poem — a fiction administered as vaccine — offers a reconstruction of the natural world from two principles, light and night.

PHAIDROS
A character who appears in Plato's two famous dialogues about love, *Phaidros* and *Symposium*. Cicadas play a central role in the first, and the playwright Aristophanes, in the latter, where he is made to tell a fable involving spherical humans and the origin of love.

DANTE GABRIEL ROSSETTI
An English Pre-Raphaelite painter and poet.

NINA SIMONE
An American jazz singer and pianist.

TEIRESIAS
A legendary Greek seer. Among his several adventures, he lived for seven years as a woman. The change occurred when he struck the skull of a copulating snake.

THALES of Miletos
A Greek philosopher, founder of the Milesian tradition of natural philosophy (which includes his student Anaximandros). Aristotle does not actually speak of *thalassa* (sea) specifically, but rather of water generally, in connexion with Thales (cf. *Metaphysics* A.3.983b20-25).

TLALOC
An Aztec rain god.

Acknowledgements

Earlier versions of these poems have been published in the following anthologies: *The Best Canadian Poetry in English* (Tightrope Books, 2010), *Best New Poets* (Samovar Press, 2009) and *Breathing Fire 2: Canada's New Poets* (Nightwood Editions, 2004). And the following journals: *The Antigonish Review, Arc, Descant, Event, The Fiddlehead, Grain, The Malahat Review, Matrix, Prairie Fire* and *PRISM international.* Thanks to all of the editors, and especially to Elizabeth Bachinsky, John Barton, Sabine Campbell, Anita Lahey, Amanda Lamarche, Ross Leckie, Sylvia Legris, Billeh Nickerson, Elizabeth Philips and Sheryda Warrener.

A very early version of "Ofelia" was performed by Alison Jutzi and directed by Eric Rose at Theatre Erindale. An unpublished part of "The Uncollected Works of Sallie Chisum" was performed by Rick Duthie for Toronto Underground Renaissance. Thanks to these three.

Work on the poems was made possible by a Pat Bevan Scholarship in Writing (from the University of Victoria), a Chalmers Professional Development Grant in Literature (from the Ontario Arts Council) and a Booming Ground Scholarship (from the University of British Columbia). Thanks to these organizations.

*

Thanks to Pat Binnersley, Mary Fournier, Georgia Geverding, Patrick Grant, Roger Nash, Rob O'Flanagan, Julian Patrick, James Reaney, Linda Rossetto, Judi Straughan and Liz Warman, for instruction and encouragement. Thanks also to Sheri Benning, Sylwia Chrostowska, Stasia Garraway and Scott McDougall, for different reasons.

Thanks to Stephen Heiti, and Sara Warren, for unconditional support.

Thanks to Heather Jessup, for the continuing (and occasionally heated) conversation about poetry, for her happy company, and for many other things.

Thanks to Matthew Heiti, my brother, oldest friend, first teacher of the imagination.

In memory of Michael Kajganich and Sue Campbell.

*

Thanks to Amy Bespflug, Lorna Crozier, Jack Hodgins, Patrick Lane, Tim Lilburn and Derk Wynand, for indispensable listening and responding.

Thanks to Don McKay, for generously editing the manuscript at Piper's Frith.

Thanks to Beth Follett of Pedlar Press and E.A. Hobart of Zab Design & Typography, for such care and diligence in publishing and designing.

Thanks to this book's editor, Jan Zwicky, for ten years of attention, for her vital and perceptive work on these poems through their various metamorphoses. I cannot thank her deeply enough.

WARREN HEITI was born in Sudbury, Ontario. He currently lives in Halifax, Nova Scotia, where he is a doctoral candidate in philosophy at Dalhousie University and a teaching fellow at the University of King's College.